THOUGHTS

BY

STEVE FRANKLIN PALMER

CheckPoint
Press

Thoughts..

..a collection of popular poems and prose

Steve Franklin Palmer

Copyright © 2013 by Steve Franklin Palmer.

All rights reserved. Printed in the United Kingdom and/or the USA / Australia / Canada / Germany / Spain / Brazil. No part of this publication may be reproduced, stored in a retrieval system, or transmitted, in any form or by any means, digital, electronic, mechanical, photocopying, recording, or otherwise, without the prior written permission of the publisher or the author(s) [as per CheckPoint Press contract terms]; except in the case of reviewers who may quote brief passages in a review.

THOUGHTS
Paperback Edition 2013
ISBN-13: 978-1-906628-56-7
Published by CheckPoint Press, Ireland
www.checkpointpress.com

This book is also available in hardcover from
CheckPoint Press

ISBN: 978-1-906628-57-4

Available from leading bookstores worldwide

www.checkpointpress.com

Foreword by Ian Dorking-Clark

I have read these poems with enjoyment, and some of them I have read again and again, and they are worth the rereading. Some of them raise themselves from simple verse into the realms of worthwhile poetry. I have read some that have clutched at my heart because of their sensitivity, their innocence, their lack of pretension and their lateral approach to emotion.

Steve Franklin Palmer has obviously put his heart and soul into his work, and I feel that in the reading of his poems many will find solace and comfort.

Definitely, a bedside book for those bleak or lonely hours when the voice of a friend is what one needs to set things in order.

Or, at those times when it would be nice to settle down with a warm and comfortable feeling; to know someone else has also experienced loss and victory: despair and ecstasy; loneliness and companionship; but has come out the other side, more in tune with themselves, and content with his or her share of this existence, their life.

Table of Contents

Helping Time to Heal	11
"Wait"	12
Thoughts	13
Let Go the Summer	14
Wait and See	15
Quiet Moments	16
Aunt Ethne	17
November Says, "Get Ready!"	18
Cliffs to Grains	20
The Garden's Guard	21
The Marriage of a Swan	22
Walk On	23
Stick to the Path	24
A Mind of Your Own	25
Hope's Window	26
Inverted Grace	27
The Golden Weave	28
The Day's Farewell	29
The Oyster of Your Soul	30
The Seeds of Faith	31
Ships	32
My Friends at Night	33
The Anniversary	34
Waiting There	35
Until We Meet Again	36
Memories through.. the Looking Glass	37
Rumours	38
With Love I let you go	39
That Special Piece of Heart	40
Crisis! What Crisis?	41
The Charity of Nature	42
Plodders	43
Broken Glass	44
The Bird with a Broken Wing	45
Insight	46
To Love a Stranger	47
The Youth in a Shop Doorway	48
Leave the Silence	50
The Wedding	51
Loving You No Less	52
Beyond Tomorrow's Land	53
Samuel	54
The Path of the Sun	55
Where There is Truly Light	56
Be Still for just a Moment	57
The Flower Beds	58
Let it Go, Let it Blow,... Let it Pass	59
Absence	60
It	61
May an Angel Speak	62
A Special Thanks	63
Who Butterfly?	64
The Cross of Friendship	65
In the Eye of a Storm	66

Little Lambs of Thought	67	*What Do You Believe?*	88
The Mind for Today	68	*Do you know it..*	
My Child is Ill	69	*when you hear it?*	89
A Little Smile	70	*These Last Few Steps*	90
It's In His Hands	71	*The Sculptor*	91
Two Feet in Sandals	72	*The Poet*	92
Other Roads	73	*Answers*	93
Make Clear the Way	74	*You are speaking..*	
An Early Parting	75	*to a Christian*	94
The Rocks that block the Way	76	*The Cost of Working for Jesus*	95
Would You Know Him..		*It is as we thought*	96
If He Came?	77	*A Last Goodbye*	97
The Pathway of Shadows	78	*The Tiny Little Prayer*	98
Gentle Hands	80	*A Christmas Gift*	99
His Hand Will Come	81	*Unbelievable Compassion*	100
He's On Your Side	82	*The Divine Poet*	101
To Forgive Divine	83	*Go with Faith*	102
Riverside Thoughts	84	*You Need to Look Further!*	103
The Traveller	85	*More Thoughts*	106
The Words My Hand..			
Just Could Not Write	87	*About the Author*	107

Thoughts

by

Steve Franklin Palmer

Helping Time to Heal

Whatever peace in life is broken,
Or cruel twist has come our way,
We have a special friend in Time,
For she takes the hurt away.
Yet we cannot hurry Time,
For no matter how we feel,
Time has to bring a gentle hand,
To the part she needs to heal.
So let calmly go the days,
To guide this gentle host,
For Time needs to find her way,
To the part that hurts the most.
As she brings a subtle healing,
Through the wisdom of her ways,
Welcome her this season,
Grasp at none of your birthdays.
If we stop to mark the calendar,
As a friend, she may prove slow;
So whilst Time performs her precious task,
Help her on by letting go.

"Wait!"

"Wait," is a word of faith,
Heard from a voice within,
When there is no direction or guidance,
Wait must suffice to begin.
"Wait," is a powerful action,
Worked whilst standing still,
"Wait," allows premeditation,
"Wait," will strengthen the will.
"Wait," is a word of command,
Sent to lighten the hour,
"Wait," is a word of wisdom,
"Wait," is a word of power.
"Wait," is a kind of protection,
Against quickening a stumble or fall,
"Wait," is a road to enlightenment,
Walked by the wisest of all.

Thoughts

Choose your thoughts selectively,
As you would choose your friends.
They have the power to set you free,
To seek out your troubles' ends.
Don't just see the worst of it,
It seldom turns out that way,
No-one knows what tomorrow brings,
It could be just your day.
You must have had the unexpected,
Turn of twist and fate,
Just as the eleventh hour approached,
When you thought it was too late.
Hanging by a slender thread,
When all the odds were down,
A power from above had deemed,
You'd land on solid ground.
So choose your thoughts most carefully,
It's your thinking you must train,
With only upward, onward dreams,
As you feed your mind again.

Let Go the Summer

The leaves are falling gently,
In their colours of yellow and brown,
Hanging on to the last,
Before finally falling down.
Each letter to the earth,
Is posted by the wind,
For nature knows just what to keep,
And what she should rescind.
Though we like to cling to warmth,
And the joy of longer days,
We need to replenish strength,
In store for winter's ways.
Let us write our own farewell,
As the fading summer goes,
Seeking a different vision,
In the way that nature shows.

Wait and See

Seek the hero who stands alone,
Not the noisy and shallow folk.
Find the seedling, fresh from birth,
Not the gnarled and knotted Oak.
Seek the quiet rivulet,
Not the wild and gushing stream,
Forget the unsought nightmare,
Wait for the vivid dream.
Find the rekindled flame,
Not the cinders or burnt out ash,
Wait for the words of wisdom,
Be protected from the rash.
Wait for the quiet enlightenment,
That uses your time to see,
Not the sudden revelation,
Or the quick discovery.
Wait for the silent event,
When your thoughts you need to align,
Watch how the river erodes,
To form the banks in her own, sweet time.
Whatever man has created,
You will find that nature is blessed,
With a sweeter wisdom and philosophy,
For she waits to work for the best.

Quiet Moments

A little restitution,
Is something we all need,
To sow a little harmony,
And I think I've found the seed.
Just to sit quite quietly,
Where some may think out loud,
I often steal a moment,
Whilst sitting in a crowd.
Like the crutches of a lame man,
My spirit needs supports,
Please leave me in those moments,
When I'm married to my thoughts.
Peace has to come from somewhere,
So I need time just to breathe,
And I'm on a private line,
Where interference makes me seethe.
Don't wonder what I'm thinking,
Or offer a penny in some jest,
I'll be with you in a moment,
When I'm feeling at my best.
Take away my good name,
And gossip if you must,
But don't take my quiet moments,
For in these I put my trust.

Aunt Ethne

Aunt Ethne will come on a Sunday,
And she'll wear a ridiculous hat.
We all have to stand and admire it,
She demands it as a matter of fact.
Just to confirm our suspicions,
Our eyes all stare at the clock.
We all but stand to attention,
When we hear that familiar knock.
There's this presence about Aunt Ethne,
I've not felt from anyone before,
Like an actress she'll make her entrance,
And then stand quite proud at the door.
She'll flash that diamond ring of hers,
And command our attention will she.
She'll tap with that silly umbrella,
Even the rain and she must agree.
If they argued, her and the weather,
I'm sure my great aunt would win.
You don't disagree with Aunt Ethne,
I'm afraid it's just not the done thing.
We use only our best bone china,
But I bet she knows we are poor,
And nobody leans on the table,
Or dares drop a crumb on the floor.
If you ever should meet our aunt Ethne,
As out walking proudly she'll go,
I'm not really afraid of the peacock,
But don't tell her I told you so.

November Says, "Get Ready!"

If you are wondering what to do,
In these November days,
Who can tell us better,
Than nature's wayside ways?
Some order must be calling,
The obedient nature wave,
For the leaves are changing colour,
In a way they should behave.
Ivy's leaves are bleaching green,
She knows what she must do,
Trailing out her dresses,
And showing them to you.
She's always one ahead of us,
And senses long before,
Refusing to procrastinate,
In time to deck our door.
Holly is pushing forward,
Boasting her green leaves,
And mistletoe is creeping,
Through the arms of resting trees.
Berries are proudly showing off,
Blushing Red they say,.
"We're here before the robin's breast,
To remind you of that day!"
Autumn has been cooling off,
For the wind is here to blow,
And the thicker green of winter,
Wears her coat to catch the snow.

Some order's calling through the air,
Giving nature some persuasion,
Commanding her to celebrate,
That celestial occasion.
Is nature to remind us,
With beauty as her power?
Are we nearly ready?
Do we know the time and hour?
Let's begin our preparation,
By straightening up today,
And set a good example too,
By following her way.

Cliffs to Grains

Cliff upon cliff came before me,
Too high and too wide to surmount,
So I stood and I stopped for a moment,
As there seemed to be no way out.
I sighed as I put my foot forward,
And rested my head in my hands,
Looking down to the ground I saw it,
The answer lay there in the sands.
Each little grain seemed to tell me,
Every piece is just part of a rock,
If you scoop to pick up a handful,
You've a key with which to unlock.
It is only by seeing the mountain,
Can you see the piece you can't climb,
But if you stop and look at each handful,
The cliffs you will walk through in time.

The Garden's Guard

In gardens that we come to,
We often find a Rose,
Before the snowy onset,
Still watching us she grows.
Showing to the winter,
Before the ground grows hard,
As if she lingered there,
To be the garden's guard.

The Marriage of a Swan

Head proud, bright eyed, in the night of her dream,
A swan glides in, to the aisle of the stream.
Bouquet waters ripple, to a hymn of the trees,
Then the song of the willows is hushed by the breeze.
She floats to the groom, the waters beside,
The down and the wings are the gown of this bride.
The moon is delighted as father this May,
For this evening is shining to give her away.
Then a waterfall organ shimmers confetti of white,
As her majesty glides off into the night.

Walk On

You've walked all amongst the wet grass,
And the clouds have been blowing by,
Though there's mud and there's puddles around you,
You feel you can let out your sigh.
Because finally there is your silver,
The streak that is shining for you,
Though more storm clouds come over,
And the sun is still farther from view.
So with head high, with step, you march bravely,
Pulling tightly the coat that you don,
Resilient to all that surrounds you,
A smile you can bravely put on.
If you feel deep down you can conquer,
And you'll let these troubles blow by,
There's more to the path that you walk in,
Than the picture you catch in your eye.

Stick to the Path

It was only the start of the winter,
Yet the grass was covered with snow,
And I sat all alone on the park bench,
For I knew not which way to go.
Then I looked up and saw some footprints,
That were left behind, although pale,
Someone in much confusion,
Had also got lost in their trail.
They had marched up and down several times,
And although it was cruel to laugh,
They had circled the distance they'd covered,
And even crossed over their path.
Amusing to look from a distance,
But any outsider could see,
If they'd kept to the path in the middle,
They'd have got where they wanted to be.
I stood up feeling more hopeful,
The folly of some folk is glee,
Until walking besides the footprints,
I discovered they belonged to me.

A Mind of Your Own

If you are to your feelings true,
Then the stronger you will be,
When what you feel, will not support,
How others want you to be.
Let your heart beat its own rhythm,
Your soul knows its own tone,
The wisest voices you will find,
Came from those who stood alone.
Listen to that quiet voice,
That's not made from the crowd,
Received within a single mind,
In a head of which you're proud.
Build a world, that's from your heart,
A mind that's of itself,
That's backed by your own reasoning,
And swayed by no-one else.

Hope's Window

In the home of disillusionment,
Walls close in on you.
Your heart gets claustrophobic,
Then how can hope get through?
Find a breathing space,
For Hope within your halls,
We often house obstructions,
Within our own high walls.
Leave an idea open,
Like a window in a tower,
Some joys come unpredicted,
As if they know their hour.
So if doors close in front of you,
And some doors close behind,
Hope can find her window still,
Somewhere in your mind.

Inverted Grace

You may have been forgiving,
With your spiritual wealth,
But does the sweetness of that mercy,
Reflect towards yourself?

The Golden Weave

There's a point in your life,
When all goodness had dropped,
You needed some help,
But nobody stopped.
When no one was good,
Circumstances were rotten,
It has stayed in your mind,
You have never forgotten.
Someone may need your help,
But why should you in turn,
Now it's somebody else?
Your anger may burn.
That choice is now yours,
To do better than they,
If you now choose the moment,
To make wiser the way.
Your mind becomes richer,
Brighter patterns unfold,
For threads spun like these,
Weave hearts made of gold.

The Day's Farewell

In the wet dew mists of the evening,
When the sun is trying to sleep,
I start to awake with the romance,
From the memories I find that I keep.
For just in her painting of evening,
Her oils have captured it all,
She knows of the sorrow of parting,
As the dew on the grass starts to form.
Foresters leave their woodlands,
As the tide starts to rest on the beach,
A dog in the distance is howling,
For his home to be well within reach.
It is sometimes my misunderstanding,
But the soul is meant to have rest,
And as the birds sing their prayers in the evening,
It would seem that nature knows best.

The Oyster of Your Soul

If truly you forget and give,
With sincere, trustworthy acts,
By nature of the grit within,
Your shell concedes the act.
With every layer your soul creates,
Your goodness must unfurl,
As deep within your kindly eyes,
Will shine a hidden pearl

The Seeds of Faith

From the field within our mind,
Weeds of doubt will often grow,
If we do not occupy
The space within the rows.
We have to raise our faith,
Or doubts that once were shallow,
Will overwhelm our minds,
When we leave them out to fallow.
Doubts will take possession
Of any lonely place,
Doubts, like gossips, feed
Upon an empty space.
So within our field of thought,
Like seedlings in a row,
We need to tend the faith,
From which good feelings grow

Ships

When you sit dreaming on the quay,
And a future hope to find,
Are there ships that need not be,
In the harbours of your mind?
Within the havens you cherish most,
Bringing comfort to the day,
Are there ships from yesteryear,
That should have sailed away?
Are there ships of bad report,
That failed life's stormy seas?
Are there boats within your mind,
That hold bad memories?
Let go the cargoes of the past,
And the ships of yesterday;
Trusting that your waves in time,
Will rock them on their way.

My Friends at Night

An orange segment was the moon,
And covered by the dark,
Then I saw them emerging,
From the middle of the park.
They winked and shimmered softly,
To earth and planet Mars,
And spoke to me that evening,
In the language of the stars.
It depends from where you're looking,
How you see things on the whole,
Your chances could look very slim,
When your moon is really full.
From where I am standing,
How small those problems are;
Set apart in darkness,
No bigger than a star.

The Anniversary

You have thought for many reflective hours,
When to my grave have brought me flowers,
But grieve not there, when it's me you miss,
Instead find peace, in the meaning of this.
Where you remember me, how can I be gone?
There in your heart, I still live on.
I can return and to you can give,
From within your memories, so let me live.
To that valley of your mind, let me arrive,
Where I did not die and am still alive,
On this anniversary, please do not weep,
For I still live on, in the memories you keep.

Waiting There

Your phone call came from out of the blue,
Just as I had forgotten, I needed to.
You went away, without a care,
And now have it in mind, to reappear.
But I am gone and you are waiting there.
You wonder why I went and where!
To another world, a light was shone,
Away from darkness, alone - but gone.
Now when your darkness, proves too great,
For your own enlightenment, you now must wait,
For this time it's your turn, and it's only fair,
That you now spend it - waiting there!

Until we meet again

Each of us may come from the same source of love as all mankind and yet, may need to flow in different directions, as if guided by some secret watershed.

Our hearts' desires must be fully explored and our souls become known by many others, for we can never be completely taught by those to whom we were earliest shown.

Most men have become wiser by testing the waters of a different spring and need to taste waters surfacing from another watering hole.

Each man must seek his own fountain of knowledge from which to drink, for we are cleansing in each of us a different soul.

Memories through the Looking Glass

Looking backwards, through the glass,
Treasuring each the gilded mile,
Searching the lane of memory,
In sadness, mellowed, I force a smile.
In tearful sentiment I search,
And greet each reflection with a sigh,
Watching the mirror frame now lovely,
Of days that make me want to cry.
I hold no treasures, such as these,
Witness the teardrop within my eye,
For there I must leave my loved ones,
In happy days gone by.

Rumours

Somewhere a rumour gets started,
Maybe of someone admired,
Then somebody overhears it,
When somebody else has enquired.
Someone tells the story,
Somebody adds on their bit,
Somebody sees something else,
That they actually think is it.
Often a storm gets brewing,
And lashes and whips of the tongue,
Uphold in a furious manner,
Just a rumour that someone begun.
Whatever you hear on the wind,
Or gets blown around on the tide,
Fail to form any judgements,
Until you've heard the other side.
Don't pass it on to the neighbours,
In that blind, repetitive shout,
Keep it within the silence,
Until the truth is worked out.

With Love I let You Go

For a while I let you in,
Just to heal and see you live,
But this is sure to help you realise,
It is in freeing that we give.
There's a pain that comes from parting,
But it's right I'm sure you know,
That anyone who wants you,
Has to love and let you go.
Despite the nurture and the loving,
You were not for me to mould,
So it's freedom that I'm giving,
For pining only keeps the hold.
I had to hear you speak it,
From the deepness of your heart,
That it's sadness I am causing,
So it's better that we part.
Many things I'd like to tell you,
Other wisdom I could show.
But if it's causing grief and sorrow,
It is with love I let you go.

That Special Piece of Heart

To stop us giving far too much,
Where a heart could soon be spent,
For our goodness' sake, we should not give,
That which was only lent.
There are some people in the world,
Who will push us far too hard,
But should never win the special heart,
Our spirit needs to guard.
Placed in store, by act of grace,
One thing our dear Lord does,
Is remind us of that piece of heart,
That He gave just for us.
If anyone then puts us down,
Or leaves us feeling bad:
We can still seek out that piece of heart,
That He gave just for us.

Crisis! What Crisis?

When the clock besides the bed,
Heralds the morning call,
We may often find on rising,
That we need not rush at all.
And so it is, in life we find,
When we hear an urgent call,
We overreact, for the circumstance,
Was no drama at all.

The Charity of Nature

Hear the birds sing,
Their sweet song of mirth,
With the help of the breeze,
To praise mother earth.
To the gentle alarm,
Of Old Father Time,
In her morning arises,
To a dawn chorus rhyme.
She bathes in the dew,
So her flowers may bloom,
Inviting that softness,
To remain in her home.
She gives to the birds,
rest in her trees,
their branches outstretched,
as they yearn just to please.
See those trees smile,
To the grass all around,
As they happily give,
Their leaves to the ground.
Let us follow then,
In the way it should be,
That we gladly give,
Of our own charity.

Plodders

Just because the road's not ended,
Where you may think it really ought,
Just because it needs more effort,
And you've not finished where you thought.
Just because the world's not ready,
To give you what you've truly earnt,
You must believe that God is working,
Where the scales of justice weren't.
Don't acquiesce the worthwhile struggle,
Futile though it's sometimes seen,
You will find you end up wondering,
What it was that might have been.
There may be more miles to walk,
Than you had really bargained for,
But don't you dare give up the struggle,
Remember you have walked far more.

Broken Glass

I came upon a lake,
In a mood that would not pass,
Where reflected sunlight danced,
As though on broken glass.
Something here arrested me,
In a need for spiritual health,
In a pulling to a path,
A reminder of the self.
To the pressures of this world,
We compromise ourselves;
Yet into the inner soul,
It seems the spirit delves.
I know I do not do,
The things I know I should;
And I know I do not work,
As I would wish I could.
In another world out there,
By the silver shimmer of streams,
I was pulled by the spirit of waters,
To the calling of my dreams.

The Bird with a Broken Wing

I opened a window one morning, to let that morning in,
With often so much to accomplish, we know not where to begin,
Providence made me look downward, and I saw a poor little thing;
Strutting and falling over, was a bird with a broken wing.
Not too bad on the face of it - still a bird with a chirp that could sing,
Stirred up by the chords of compassion, I had to take that bird in.
I believe that the sick in spirit have a right to their dignity, too;
I sensed that the bird was so damaged, as its mind had been broken in two.
Its sick, sad eyes had told me - although it had spoken no word -
Its nestling life had been shattered. It was the saddest song I had heard.
And in its own frustration, it would often peck at me,
Biting the hand that fed it. What was it I could not see?
The temptation then was to cage it, and to make it heal right through,
And to force it food and guidance; what was I to do?
It had caused us both more anguish, throughout my sheltered reign,
Because its way was so damaged, it would steal anodyne for its pain.
Then a voice from within said wisely, 'Let it go, let it go, say goodbye."
For not until heaven is ready, will that bird be able to fly.

Insight

Where the medicine in one man's mind,
Meets with the wounds in another's
And crosses the un-bridgeable gap-
And heals.
Like the gentle touch of angels
It is there in a world above judgement,
Twinned beside this one
As if in party,
To a fifth dimension.

To Love a Stranger

Please forgive me for my fear, I don't mean to show resistance;
But I have to feel this love from the safety of this distance,
For some blind and foolish reason, I find I start to shake,
If one step in my direction you physically take.
Your absolutely silent eyes can seem to say so much;
How dare you stand so close? What if we accidentally touch?
That curious glance you send is like a message left unsigned -
And when you see me look away, what thoughts go through your mind?
I hope I'd find you dream - as I so often do -
When you glance those eyes at me, and I steal these eyes from you;
Of how life could be between us, if our lives we could restart,
Were our circumstances different - free to listen to the heart.
But as they say, "The caged bird sings, from a very glorious pain'
And in this unfulfilled romance, as such it must remain'
As a golden precious memory, shared just between we two;
For sadly in this real world, no dream like this comes true.

The Youth in a Shop Doorway

Two large eyes emerged from a sleeping bag I did not see,
I was arrested by that moment, in uncontrollable empathy;
Not the son of anyone, just the open world his teacher,
But those great large eyes affixed to mine,
That was the humbling feature.
Acknowledging the pain, above which we try to rise,
A curious "from- the -eyes" concern
No convention can disguise.
Scars are left and blemishes, only an inner eye can see;
We were exchanging our compassion,
That's what he gave to me.
Reassurance felt, as days went by,
                              though he'd no social role;
He was serving a different purpose;
The deepening of his soul.
We were sharing hidden assonance
                              whilst that look to me he gave
Compelled, he even dropped his guard,
So important was his gaze.
His curious, confusing glance, that I could not quantify,
Became obscured by living bushes,
Of people passing by.
The action of a courageous gent, of genuine concern,
Was taking him some purchased food
But those eyes to me returned.
The kindness of strangers walking, on which he had relied;
Not worthy hear of doctrine,
He was the better qualified.

The uncomfortableness of feeling,
                          of that glance he gave to me;
I knew he recognised, there was pain enough for three.
A presence of the familiar
From a heart that was worldly-wise
As if he knew in depth, from the memory of my eyes.
Stirred by this very moment, I received a message sent,
For I felt within my soul,
That silent compliment.
I know I "kind-of-know", and I knew he "Kind-of-knew"
That in our own quiet way,
We would try to make it through.
The spirit of that moment, from our plane is quite diverse:
Perceived in a fifth dimension-
A parallel universe.
A brief but strange encounter, in a secret hidden glance
Viewed from a concrete pavement
Of abnormal circumstance.

Leave the Silence

We need to hear ourselves,
For listening is the key;
So if you find a place of silence
Please leave it - let it be.
For holy is the silence,
And good it is, if left,
For he who takes the silence,
Commits sacrilege and theft.
We need to keep our quiet,
To hear those inner rings;
For they clarify our thoughts
And other sacred things.
If you would hear that voice,
To know what true wealth really is-
Just listen to the silence,
For the richness heard is His.
Silence nurtures wisdom
At its own un-hurried pace;
And it so becomes the man,
Who leaves silence in its place

The Wedding

A gateway opened from heaven,
And a light now shines upon,
A very special pledge,
To where their hearts are coming from.
Now bound within its force,
May a deeper love begin,
In their public declaration,
Of something felt within.
What privilege they have brought us,
As though guided from above,
Just to bask within the light,
Of their very special love.
In a prayer from the heart,
May their path be blessed and even,
And their wedding prove to be,
A marriage made in heaven.

Loving you no less

To keep the peace of friends,
As they try to play their part,
I don't always share the feeling,
That sits quietly in my heart.
Just to keep things moving,
I put on some kind of show,
They think I should be over you,
And yet, how can they know?
To keep my thoughts at bay,
I employ some kind of ban.
I try to keep so busy,
Or as busy as I can.
Sure, I have my life together,
In some order and assembly,
But some old familiar cue,
Will trigger off some memory.
I just have to face the fact,
As your memory comes again,
I'm loving you still now,
No less than I did then.

Beyond Tomorrow's Land

I need not fear tomorrow,
for tomorrow has only the familiar worries of today.
And if I choose to take an intrepid path, all may be lost,
that I have come safely to outstay.
Invisible to the eye, came a cue, sent to move;
a journey long that spoke of promised love.
Someone immortal has paved a way before me though,
for I know I must tread these cobbles alone.
If I waiver or falter, please do not fear,
and rush to steady my hand.
It is because I have seen into a world beyond tomorrow.
I have seen into a beautiful land.

Samuel

There's a little boy called Samuel,
Who lives at number six,
You have to be pretty clever,
To catch him at his tricks.
He plays with all his dinner,
And still plays when this is through,
You better move that ashtray,
Oh! and your coffee too.
He pulls away the aerial,
From mum's television box,
She tries in vain to stop him,
But he's mischief from his socks.
We call him, "fingers everywhere,"
'cause they're where the action's at.
Oh blimey, now he's off again,
"Samuel! Don't touch that!"
He only stands just so high,
Though we tell him "No!" from the start,
His face just beams with innocence,
With a smile to break your heart.
Though he's only just learnt to walk,
Everywhere he has to roam,
"There he is the little tyke."
"Samuel, leave that alone!"
I don't know when he'll learn from us,
How not to be so wild,
Yet despite his little impish ways,
He's a very special child.

The Path of the Sun

The sun of the summer,
Is a welcoming light,
Warming our hearts,
When reaching its height,
Spreading its confidence,
With no doubt to its role,
Raising our spirits,
And touching the soul.
Let us learn from its rays,
To believe we can win.
With no fear of failure,
When it's summer within.

Where there is Truly Light

Looking downward is a habit,
When our world is in turmoil,
We seem to look for solace,
Upon the barren soil.
When our path is overshadowed,
and we know not what to pray,
We need only gaze upon the skies,
Of any darkened way.
When we look toward the heavens,
We find we have no doubt,
For faith is all around us,
If we only seek it out.
For the power of the heavens,
Will warm our hearts and guide them,
As miracles can't be hidden
When we have the faith to find them.

Be Still for just a Moment

If you're still for just a moment,
With just a pause to blink,
And listen to your inner voice,
As you allow yourself to think.
From deep within, a thought begins,
Just by sitting there,
A picture starts to form itself,
Though you know not from where.
If you're still for just a moment,
And let the outer world go by,
Relax yourself on where you are,
And hear the inner cry.
The voice inside will tell you,
Your cares will pass away,
If only you can plan,
The path that goes that way.

The Flower Beds

This is an array of yellow carnations. I hope you like flowers.

Although I cannot create like the gardener with the immortal hand, I can nurture seedlings to growth. Nature needs help and we the catalysts need it too.

Like a flower in the wind, you can lead to the elements and dance, be part of the crowd when it's going your way and when the wind gets too strong, protect yourself.

When we lose touch with our own souls, like the flower beds, we need restoring.

Refrain with your own peace. Shelter and remain in touch with yourself.

Nothing in nature's beauty is sudden. It needs some rain to water it, wind to give it life and then time to bloom.

If you can bide with the gardener for a while, like the flower-beds, you too can blossom.

Let it go, let it blow, let it pass.

Let that storm blow over you now,
It has gone and has done its last.
Whatever it was, it was and has gone,
It has raged, let it blow, let it pass.
If you weep too deep, a scar may be formed,
Whatever the cause or the deed,
And refrain from rubbing the sore,
As a wound it can only bleed.
Let it float unto heaven and away from you,
As a bubble of trouble, that has shown.
Let the world see you then, at your very best,
When to the clouds, it has gone and has blown.

Absence

There are times when I feel you're not with me,
Though my heart tries to tell me it's so,
I wish I didn't feel this loneliness,
I wish I felt you wouldn't go.
There are times when I need you near me,
And they are always when you feel gone,
I wish for the world you'd be with me.
To help me feel, I'd go on.

'IT'

Let it now be over,
And at last be done,
You have carried your cross,
Like the chosen one.
Their minds have worked,
To bring this fall,
Yet in his way,
God loves them all.
And so you must,
In kind reflect,
Not allow your soul,
This sad neglect.
Realise here,
Where the thorns begun,
So if you can forgive,
Consider it done.

May an Angel Speak

Through an angel's voice,
We sometimes hear,
God's sound advice,
As a song in the air.
So may you listen,
That He may prove,
That in their light,
The dark must move.
And may his words,
Shine out somewhere,
And an angel speak,
Of you in prayer.

A Special Thanks

I said a prayer to Jesus,
To thank him for you friend,
I thought to pray for many things,
But did not in the end.
As I lit a special candle,
And placed it in its bowl,
The gentle flame enlightened me,
I felt it in my soul.
So instead I shared my feelings,
And the love I've known with you,
Although I felt He understood,
Before my prayers were through.
I could have asked for wealth,
And all that it stands for,
But as my treasure's knowing you,
I cannot ask for more.

Who Butterfly?

Whose loving hands abandoned laws,
And nurtured your design,
No artist claiming freedom,
Could shave those wings that fine.
What fine fate of loveliness,
Could guide the path your thoughts possess?
Who's granted you the privilege?
Whose love has let you go?
You justify by beauty,
The dance of your own show.
There's no such greatness in man's art.
Who had the soul? Who had the Heart?
If dominion stands for liberty,
Why do we have less than thee?
Who Butterfly? Who Butterfly?
Had grace to grant such wings,
To fly the paths of liberty,
Unruled by other beings?
Some inner peace has helped you by,
But who has licensed you to fly?
I only hope I get to see,
The Master who created thee.

The Cross of Friendship

Often in times of trouble,
To see we don't completely fail,
It seems that unseen forces,
Are at work behind a veil.
For each committed Christian,
May find he stumbles too.
Yet a hand is somehow sent,
Someone brings us through.
So that cross upon the hillside,
Should not bring us shame,
When we know we still are trying,
And calling on His name.
We still have a gentle guardian,
For that cross was not His end,
So may it serve instead to teach us
That in Him we have a friend.

In The Eye of a Storm

Without a gap, between the thoughts,
Within your troubled mind,
How can the Lord send comfort,
Unless a space He finds?
That break within the turmoil,
To renew your strength to sail,
Onwards through the waters,
Of any full blown gale.
Find a space of silence,
Within its raging harm,
Make an eye within the storm,
Some space of peace and calm.

Little Lambs of Thought

Little lambs of thought,
Often go out to stray,
Taking our minds to problems,
That cannot be solved by day.
So the evening rest of sleep,
May bring its own insight,
As sleep brings opportunity,
For The Shepherd to guide at night.
Anxiety is but Peace's way,
Of folding her dreams upon their way;
Pointing lambs, in tomorrows light,
That seemed so lost, in the dark of night,
Yet destined to find their way.

The Mind for Today

There are times in one's life when to prosper,
You must keep each day apart,
Dealing only with what the day offers,
And nurturing some faith in your heart.
Sufficient to the day is the evil therein,
Or so our religion may say,
So pray for the help you are needing,
Only to challenge this day.
No one knows the time or the hour,
And you will only have wasted that day,
If anxious for what tomorrow brings,
Your problems have been called away.
For many a trial has finished,
By the act of a fate that is kind,
And many a crisis you'll discover,
Has only been lived in your mind.

My Child is Ill

I pray you're watching over Lord,
Just to keep us feeling good,
For at times like these I weaken,
As any parent would.
Day by day I've loved him,
Before that time that he first smiled,
And although he's now a grown up,
To my heart he's still that child.
He has added to my life Lord,
In the way you'd wish he would,
And I'd give instead my life,
If needed that I should.
I wait to hear in patience,
As many prayers are said,
For you dear Lord to tell me,
What I must do instead.
I just pray to see him well again,
Please speed along that day,
For no effort is spared hourly,
Nor no price too great to pay.

A Little Smile

Friends like you are special,
And have rarely come my way,
So I took a little trouble,
To make the time to pray.
I asked God to bring you joy,
From a loving point of view,
And to bring a little happiness,
In just a day or two.
So if you feel a little lift,
And can read this with a smile,
God has answered this, my prayer,
In such a little while.

It's In His Hands

I said a prayer to Jesus,
To place you in His hands,
And asked if He would help you,
To carry through your plans.
Though I sensed no need to tell Him,
Or to bring Him up to date,
It seems He knew you'd carry,
Only so much weight.
So just in case you worry,
How far the problem spans,
Remember in my prayer,
I have placed you in His hands.
The shoulders that withstood the whips,
And took the cross on too,
And the palms that bore the nails,
Are now to carry you.
He's sure about your problems,
And knows where to begin,
So feel your burden lifting now,
I have given it to Him.

Two Feet in Sandals

I wandered in search of the peaceful,
And found myself starting to dream,
Joining the path beside me,
Was the breath and calm of the stream.
Kneeling besides the waters,
A reflection I squinted to see.
A figure in white robes was standing,
With two feet in sandals by me.
Turning slowly, I looked for the vision,
But saw nothing and only a voice,
In a gentleness seeing confusion,
Said, true life was a multiple choice.
"I have come, my child, to free you,
No one is bound to begin,
I have taken this away from you,
Now search for the beauty within."
Still amazed by the blessing that happened,
All that remained to be seen,
In the pathway that leads to the river,
Were prints where two sandals had been.

Other Roads

God won't be guided,
God won't be led,
Patiently waiting,
Follow instead.
Those nagging questions,
That flow through the brain,
Leave in abeyance,
Till He comes back again.
Don't hurry your Lord,
Be patient instead,
Not all of his pathways,
Come straight to your head.
Wait to be guided,
Down those other roads too,
Be patiently waiting,
When He comes back to you.

Make Clear the Way

Another day's dawning,
That, I must go through,
Dear Lord go before me,
In all that I do.
Let not my failed yesterdays,
Drag this day down,
Allowing tomorrows,
In their time to come round.
It is not always easy,
To know what is good,
Or to carry through living,
In the way that I should.
So in all that I meet,
As I go through my day,
Pass there before me,
And make clear the way.

An Early Parting

We wish you could have stayed with us,
We would have liked you here,
But the angels came so suddenly,
And took you to their care.
In the gardens of the heavens,
Growing with Jesus' loving care,
Look down upon us sometimes,
The family you left here.
We could not find the reasons,
And never within our time,
Will understand God's seasons,
That reap before the prime.
One by one we'll join you,
And maybe then we'll see,
The reason why, out God above,
Allowed what was to be.

The Rocks that Block the Way

When the candles keep going out,
And you feel you're about to fail,
Know a flame is burning somewhere,
Hidden beyond a vale.
Obscured by the darkness,
Where mountains block the view,
See these only as the mountains,
He wants to guide you through.
Each step, each stone, each heartache,
Leads beyond this rocky path,
You have to tread to happiness,
To the many joys He hath.
All we seem to see at times,
Is the gloom within the day,
But the Lord can see your future,
Beyond the rocks that block the way.

Would You Know Him, if He Came?

If Jesus were alive today,
Born of another birth,
No angels to herald His coming,
And He walked upon the earth;
If He were in your street today,
Or praying in a pew,
Would you know Him if He came,
And walked right up to you?
If Jesus were alive today,
Would there be any change?
Would He fit the face of fashion,
Or would He look a little strange?
Would He wear the clothes we're wearing?
Would He walk the way we choose,
Or be with the poor and homeless,
With nothing more to lose?
Would you know Him if He came,
From the life He had before,
If He asked you for some water,
When He knocked upon your door?
Would you ask Him for a miracle?
And would you let out a sigh;
If when you felt that presence,
He went and passed you by?
In case we meet with Jesus,
Let us remember this,
As surely this is one man,
We would not want to miss,
Let us treat then, each person,
As the Son of God to be,
If what we do to others,
We do also unto He?

The Pathway of Shadows

In the shadowy, sunlit forest, I confronted many glades. Venturing forward, I brushed harshly past some bushes and arrestingly, they caught my arms.

I had not expected such severe scratches or piercings.

Instinctively, I grabbed at the green leaves of some plant, that they might serve as an anodyne for relief.

They could have been the leaves of weeds, yet in that sightless pain and panic, their coolness healed and I proceeded on the greenest grasses of an untrodden way which lead blindly, deeper into the forest.

A shallow patch of mud was deeper than I believed. Underfoot it brought a slip, thoughts as erratic as the wind and then panic. It took all I had to keep balance, arms reaching out to keep my weight even. There was no clearness of thought, all logic disappearing in the hundred babbles of the nearby brook.

Mercifully, my fall was broken by the grasses underneath. What fool would not have checked his steps.

I would have turned left or right for safer terrain, but the voice leading me on, kept in tune as if by some invisible force, able to bring a final silence to the heart, for the sights it led me to were beautiful. Yellow daffodils nodding in a breeze, approving, almost guiding my feet; snowdrops bowing in cool modesty, alighting the way to the seduction of bluebells ahead. The green moss, carpeted the contented rocks and stones. They were too wise to move, having found an eternal resting place. I could hear the sound of birds that had made their nests, telling as much too any creature that would listen. They had found their homes. Nothing is perceived with greater clarity in nature's voices, than the tuning it brings to the mind. This was a paradise, lost to the men of the world.

Turning around, I looked back. Amongst thorns, slippery mud and broken grasses, I had walked a straight path.

Turning again then onward, in dazzling splendour, the sun shone brightly upon a sudden mountain. It was casting a rich shadow.

As if receiving a blessing from God. It looked strong and firm in His love. I realised, for the first time ever, how black it can seem, when we walk so closely beside the Lord. Anything truly great, will cause darkness, be it of simple earth or the powerful complex love from heaven. The more solid a love is, the deeper will its shadow be.

Gentle Hands

I prayed openly to Jesus,
To guide you through these sands,
And because I prayed sincerely,
I prayed with gentle hands.
I sensed He was approaching,
To help to put things right,
As my gentle hands were working,
Inviting in His light.
For when we pray to Jesus,
And do not make demands,
Our minds are far more open,
To accept the way He plans.
Because I prayed so openly,
You now have His wisdom too,
So may God work His will with Jesus,
With the gentle hands of you.

His Hand will Come

When a storm is brewing,
And the winds are raw,
When turbulence comes,
Like never before.
If we pray, He descends,
To the flock that He keeps,
And He shepherds calm thoughts,
To reach His lost sheep.
Just clasp both your hands,
When your faith starts to drift,
Make ready your heart,
And wait for His gift.
He can never forget,
What a prayer means to some,
Just hold on and believe,
For His hand will come.

He's on Your Side

Sometimes, something difficult,
Brings itself to view,
And we need some extra help,
With what life may bring us to.
So I said a prayer to Jesus,
To help you with this task,
Because I find Him wisest,
And I only have to ask.
So let your mind be ready,
For His voice to be your guide,
For you're with the safest person,
Whilst He is on your side.
Please do not be disheartened,
Or pay heed to the rest,
For the Lord is moving in your life,
And surely He knows best.

To Forgive Divine

More than you know this has hurt me!
For my enemies now I must pray,
Dear Lord lead me on through this valley,
And your angels watch o'er me each day.
More than you know, you have wounded!
I can feel all the rage in me burn!
May God teach me here of forgiveness,
Very easy, but now it's my turn.
I feel I have lost my compassion,
This must be a trial in my fate,
May God send my discord in remission,
And all of my love back from hate.
Dear Lord all my hurting's embrace,
Whilst I pray for my feelings to lift,
And may God grant me to you by His grace,
A forgiveness that comes as His gift.

Riverside Thoughts

Surrounded by the cluttering,
Of your fellow men,
It's difficult, to find a space,
For God to speak again.
Seek out some restful waters,
Away from all around,
Find a place quite peaceful,
Near a river's ground.
The calming words of God,
In the way, they need to be,
Make a river in the mind,
To flow in harmony.
Mental healing has to come,
In a wise reflective tide,
Of quiet thoughts from God,
When by a riverside.

The Traveller

As dusk was falling, a traveller walked along the road side hoping to get a lift from a passer-by. The more he walked, the more he thought and the more he thought the more he walked and nobody stopped.

As he hurried along his way, the darkness loomed. He mused over the Lord's way and recalled that in many events throughout time, the Lord had always appeared to reverse conventional wisdom. "Good" had come from Nazareth, and the wise men had journeyed "from" the east. The Lord had always shown goodness in such an unpredictable manner. Even the writing's of the saints had left some confusing translation arguments. It seemed as if He had left even the righteous fallible. Could anyone then rely upon the Lord to show them anything clearly through anyone else?

The traveller's aching feet had walked miles and still no passer-by stopped. He continued walking and thinking until finally, he lost the Lord to his own confusion. Suddenly, like an idea from the skies it hit him! He had not prayed to the Lord about his current difficulty. So he stopped and first asked the Lord's forgiveness for his cursory thoughts and then worded his own, slow and silent prayer. As each word was uttered, the traveller felt instinctively that the Lord would answer.

About twenty-five steps later, the most luxurious transport stopped. The traveller had thirty-five miles to go, and it transpired that his host was going to the end of his road.

It concerned the traveller slightly, that in the height of his doubt, the Lord should have answered his prayer when previously, many prayers uttered in faith, had fallen to the ground. So the Lord answered to his mind. "My child, I am so pleased that you responded with a prayer for me to answer when you did - for it was then, that I most feared that I would lose you!"

The Words My Hand Just Could Not Write

I remember my hand going to my head,
My eyes wide open I could not keep.
So I did not work, but dreamed instead,
As I slowly drifted into sleep.
Then it was, a hand descended,
Shining, glowing with brilliant light,
And more conveniently, than intended,
It took my pen and began to write.
It seems some unheard voice was calling,
The hand obeyed it from afar,
I saw a drop of blood then falling,
From the centre of a scar.
Looking from my sleepy distance,
The hand was pierced that I could see,
And quite clearly, whilst the wrist danced,
The wound from a nail was shown to me.
With this hand my mind was smitten,
Much it wrote and did not cease,
In its blood, a full stop written,
A sentence said, "Now sleep in peace!"
That hand and pen would not diminish,
For I could not see my writing through.
It seems that heaven, had come to finish,
The works my hand just could not do.

What Do You Believe?

When too many beliefs confront you,
Overwhelmed by the flood of their seas,
Sail only to know your own mind,
You may not see what another man sees.
The actions of men differ widely,
When another belief here is shown,
But steer with the ark you've been given,
You need only account for your own.
For each man must meet something different,
And if only the seas were so paved,
To know when to rudder our brothers,
And to know when to part, like the waves.
You may sail where another man swam,
Or even run where another man trod,
But with peace each man in his way,
Finds hope with his version of God.

Do you know it when you hear it?

Is it present, now you're older, or was it only in your youth?
Does He talk to you through others now, within their spoken truth?
Do you know it when you hear it? Does it sound to you that true?
Do you know the voice of God, when He tries to speak to you?
Do you praise him once you've heard it, somewhere in your mind?
Does He send a little gift? Does He speak to you in kind?
If it's there within a verse, that someone else has bought,
Do you sometimes think you hear it, in that wise reflective thought?
If He wants a small donation, do you act the way you should?
Do you acknowledge and give gladly, because it feels so good?
Or does He rarely ask for money, just a service you've to do?
Do you hear the voice of God when He tries to ask of you?
Do you want an instant answer, when in prayer you've quietly sat?
Or do you expect it sometimes later, in a letter on the mat?
And if that prayer gets answered, does your head gladly nod?
Is it there within your quietest thoughts, that still small voice of God?

These Last Few Steps

As a soul on many pathways,
That brought troubles in their wake,
The end is just in sight my child,
Though you've a few more steps to take.
My two pierced feet will guide you,
Though they may walk in hidden depths.
Just believe that they can show you,
How to take these last few steps.
And know I go before you,
Though you may not always see,
That the journey you are sharing,
Is also confronting me.
And know you are no burden,
So put your mind at rest,
And be happy just to follow,
Your heart says who knows best.
For you will see me waiting,
In your future promised land,
Let me walk the way before you,
And leave my footprints in your sand.

The Sculptor

When the master hammers his sculpture,
Many Strange shapes start to form,
He bangs and He chips with His chisel,
As each stroke from His heart is torn.
For there in His mind is an image,
Obscure and kept from us all;
And as master of that which He's making,
He must stop now and then, to recall.
He knows it is worthy of earnest,
Yet pieces fall off in dismay;
We think that the pettiest pieces
He has wasted and chiselled away.
Many times when the Master is working,
We can't see the reason why;
Yet that which looks ugly from our side
Must have beauty beheld in His eye.
There seem to be jagged pieces
Where smooth loving curves we could see;
Leave Him with the tools for tomorrow
And just wait for what is to be.

The Poet

What more indulgence is here than this,
Than the arrogance of a poet's bliss,
For he spins out words, almost of song,
To a spirit within, where meanings belong.
There's an inner magic when you hear the sound,
Of rhyme and rhythm where the stanzas abound,
For quickly his inspiration has come,
And in words you'll hear what his soul has sung,
To find the privilege reserved for a sage,
Just listen to the words thrown on the page,
Captured and ringing like the bells of time,
In the miracles of an expedient rhyme.

Answers

When thoughts keep on circling,
And get stuck in your head,
In that turbulent confusion,
Look around you instead,
It may seem impossible,
In conclusion to nod,
But wild racing thoughts,
Are not answers nor God.
Not always to mind,
Will answers be placed,
As often solutions,
Stare us in the face.
Troubles when deepened,
Require stronger relief,
But you find His true answers,
Take stronger belief.

You are Speaking to a Christian

This Cross is like a testament,
From the day I first believed,
Of my partnership with Jesus,
And the things we have achieved.
Do not think that I am perfect,
Or entirely free from sin;
Just a witness to His mercy
So we can be born again.
If I look at my Cross often,
Or clutch it whilst I pray,
May it serve as a reminder,
That He brought me to this day.
I know His grace and favour,
And I mean no farce or show;
I just bear my cross with pride,
For I would like the world to know.

The Cost of Working for Jesus

The price that's paid is never lost,
Or taken by way of greed,
But to broaden by tasting other worlds,
The sense in a loving creed.
Whatever you give up for God,
Is only loaned away,
And gone to the home of another soul,
To come back another day.
Never will an act of Kindness,
Go unnoticed from above,
You might have given all you can,
And suffered for the sake of love.
But there does come a day you'll feel,
When to heart, body and soul,
Comes a love that goes beyond all price,
With the peace that's been foretold.

It is As We Thought

Death blooms as a rose within the night,
How out of season and how unright.
Unless to heaven for a moment or two,
We try to reach the golden view.
From a distant plane of higher thought,
We may hear a voice that comes unsought.
Through our distress and turbulence,
Grief may be stopped for it may make sense.
In our journey here, to piece things through,
We must put our faith in a higher view,
No mortal alone, can make this right,
We need the gift of the golden light.
In a conduit from a wiser plane,
We must turn our trust to the light again,
And wait for the voice that comes unsought,
Our grief to ease, for it is as we thought.

A Last Goodbye

Though happily each year had begun,
I had to die whilst very young.
It is so long since our last touch,
And I miss your presence there so much.
Of many things I needed to learn,
So to this place, God made me turn.
Yet with so many things to do,
I have taken this moment, to speak to you.
The life that was, was not to be mine,
Yet within this world, it has worked out fine,
Where I am now, I have found new friends,
In a place called Heaven, where the spirit ascends.
Straight to this world, few pass it by,
And no one here can really die.
Although your child you cannot see,
I know you'd be so proud of me.
I look forward to when I'll see you Mum,
So until it is your time to come,
Enjoy your life and please don't cry,
I just came to say, a last goodbye.

The Tiny Little Prayer

It came upon your soul,
In a way you could not bear,
You spoke tiny words of utterance
You thought He would not hear.
And because you spoke with love,
Whilst your faith was in reverse,
Your prayer flew straight to Heaven,
And it shook the universe.
If only you could know,
How He wanted you to start;
And if only you could see,
How it lit up in His heart!
The grit within each word,
In his protective shell is pearled'
And is as welcome in His arms
As a new born babe into the world.
He knows with deepest love,
Of all it means to you,
And will not trivialise an answer,
Whilst He takes the long term view.
He will transcend in thought,
The deepest wisdom there can be,
For your prayer has found a faithful heart,
To rest in utterly.

A Christmas Gift

This great day is a blessing mixed,
As each try to play their part,
For often a quiet loneliness,
Sits aching in the heart.
Empty spaces of absent ones,
As Christmas comes again,
And friends imposing cheerfulness,
May not feel the pain.
But accept this special spirit,
And let the gift of memory reign,
For within this gracious gift,
He lends them back again.
Christmas has a joyful message,
When His memory is our way,
For memories are the gift of God,
That are with us every day.

Unbelievable Compassion

Rage nearly stole my mercy,
I was weakening in each joint;
My heart then, too, had faltered,
For I had reached a breaking point.
Then an amazing flash of brilliance,
In a conduit shining bright,
Brought unbelievable compassion,
In a shower of heavenly light.
From a desperate plea of mercy,
Heaven now seemed to say;
Accept power from the kingdom,
Just - bask and take this ray.
Beyond all human endeavour,
From a source I cannot impart,
An unbelievable compassion,
Was forged into my heart.
A reflected love from heaven,
Now takes me through each day;
May unbelievable compassion,
Be bestowed on you one day.

The Divine Poet

We think it's we who plan,
To make our movements rhyme,
But the Lord writes for us a piece,
Decades ahead of time.
He places a poet's verse
Just waiting to be read,
As if a hand so special,
Could write that far ahead.
Know, in that special moment,
Where you had to think things through,
Whilst warmth was in your heart,
Your hand was guided, too.

Go with Faith

Go with faith, through the turbulence,
To meet your greatest need;
Go with the flow of providence,
No matter where it leads.
Go, though the storms blow harder,
Where confusing winds may howl;
Go, though you find less peace,
And much beyond control.
Go with the gushing torrents,
Though you feel about to drown;
Go with the voice of providence
Though it seems to let you down.
Go, for an order is calling,
From a channel you cannot see;
Go, though much is illusive,
For your logic's the enemy.
Go though the current of circumstance
Seems ever to take you in;
Go - down that great uncharted way,
Where the end is about to begin.

You Need to Look Further!

You thought that you had gone far enough; you thought that no one could possibly go beyond this point, no one could possibly stay the distance and survive; well, you are wrong. You need to look further! You need to look beyond yourself, your world, your place, your dwelling and the very fabric of your being. You need to look further!.

You need to look without effort, you need to relax into looking, for only in the surprise of the meeting with another can you see yourself through them. You need to look further and they will help you look. For just as they disarm you, so you may surprise them and you will both wonder what it is that you are looking at. Yet you need to look further!

You need to go beyond sense for what is sense. Sense has only taken you to this point, so you need to look further! It is no good wearing a fine coat either. A fine coat, even the very finest, will not hide what you need to sees. It is somewhere halfway between a sense and a feeling; it is not of this world and so you need to look further. It is no good going inside of yourself for it is inside of yourself that only another can see what you need to see in order to go further. It is many miles along the route of the soul, this is not far enough, and you need to go further. It is no good going only to the point of despair for that is a route well travelled and it is not far enough for you to gain the road across and out of it. You need to look further! You need to go beyond your usual route of understanding, for your usual route of understanding is a fake, it isn't good enough, you will need to look further! You will need to look beyond: Yes! Way, way beyond that which you normally see and when you think that that is far enough surely, no! No! It isn't, you will need to look further!

You will need to look further! For to find this special person, the one that you know is already in existence somewhere in your heart and please God somewhere out there also: the one with the key to your doorway to the world of the mysterious, missing link for which you are prepared to go further, you will find, you will need to look further!

Yes, you need to look further, for the man with the missing piece, the man with the extra special gifts, is already well known to you and is never going to leave you unaided in your quest, for he is just as earnestly seeking you as you are seeking him and yet despite this awesome majesty, you will find that you will need to look further!

You can only find him in another human being for this is a chemistry that can only exist on love and nothing can destroy this living, breathing, overpowering chemistry more surely than a hand and heart, that is set alone in the darkness; just waiting, so closely, so near to hand all the time, in your mind and thoughts, growling disquiet to all peace that would lead you away from your quest. This is your enemy and is so close to you that you can hear him so often without the need for peace and quiet. He is the closest shadow on the soul.

This is why you will need to look further!

Still further, for a mirror and a window both: An uncomfortable and yet comforting burden of enlightenment; a hard day's work and light toil too. He is crystal clear and paradox both, he is indescribable and easy to speak of and just as you think you have got to know him, you will feel that there is still one more page at least yet to be read, to be shared and kept at the same time. He is just amazing! You feel you are just about to meet him, don't you? You think I am going to tell you where to find him; you think I know where that man is most surely to be found because I have made you feel that he is now closer. Well, he is closer, because your pointer is now towards him and you can in some sense feel a sense of this majesty but this is not far enough you know. No, even from this point you must travel, my wary friend, for if you truly want to find him; you will need to look further!

More Thoughts

Release
If your love is so selfish it imprisons someone, your dark desire is to make them look bad and you want to keep a hold; then your love becomes your prison too, and your heart is the only window through which there is release.

To Forget
One of the most graceful lanes upon the route of memory, is the road marked - "To forget."

About the Author

Steve Franklin Palmer was born in 1958 at Guist, Norfolk, the forth of eight children. He was educated at Fakenham Secondary Modern and later attended the Norfolk College of Arts and Technology in King's Lynn. He has worked as an actor, and model. He moved to Norwich in 1993, and currently lives in Halstead in Essex.

Thank you for reading Steve Franklin Palmer's book of poems. If you would like to follow more of Steve's work, please refer to the link below.

Steve Franklin Palmer

www.stevefranklinpalmer.moonfruit.com

www.ingramcontent.com/pod-product-compliance
Lightning Source LLC
LaVergne TN
LVHW011427080426
835512LV00005B/308